Outlearning the Wolves

Surviving and Thriving in a Learning Organization

by David Hutchens

illustrated by Bobby Gombert

third edition
with a foreword by Robert Fritz

 PEGASUS COMMUNICATIONS, INC.

Waltham

Outlearning the Wolves: Surviving and Thriving in a Learning Organization
by David Hutchens; illustrated by Bobby Gombert
Copyright © 1998, 2000, 2007 by David Hutchens
Illustrations © 1998 Pegasus Communications, Inc.

Library of Congress Cataloging-in-Publication Data
Hutchens, David.
Outlearning the wolves: surviving and thriving in a learning organization / by David Hutchens; illustrated by Bobby Gombert—3rd ed.
p.   cm.
ISBN 978-1-883823-16-0   (1-883823-16-1)
1. Organizational learning—Problems, exercises, etc.   I. Title.
HD58.82.H88   1998
658.4'06—DC21   97-53299
CIP

Acquiring editor: Kellie Wardman O'Reilly
Project editor: Lauren Johnson
Production: Boynton Hue Studio and Nancy Daugherty

♻ Printed on recycled paper.
Printed in the United States of America.
First printing, March 1998.

Pegasus Communications, Inc. is dedicated to providing resources that help people explore, understand, articulate, and address the challenges they face in managing the complexities of a changing world. Since 1989, Pegasus has worked to build a community of systems thinking and organizational development practitioners through newsletters, books, audio and video tapes, and its annual *Systems Thinking in Action*® Conference and other events.
For more information, contact us at:

Pegasus Communications, Inc.
One Moody Street
Waltham, MA 02453-5339
Phone: (800) 272-0945 / (781) 398-9700
Fax: (781) 894-7175
Email: customerservice@pegasuscom.com   info@pegasuscom.com

www.pegasuscom.com

5854
        12   11   10   09   6   5   4   3   2

For Robbie

Foreword by Robert Fritz

Wisdom, combined with wit and charm, is rare indeed. How wonderful to come across these qualities in the pages of *Outlearning the Wolves*, as we follow the exploits of a flock of sheep confronting an age-old problem: a pack of wolves. What should they do as their friends disappear one by one? In the beginning of the story, the sheep find many reasons to simply accept the status quo. Without significant change, their numbers continue to diminish, and it seems that nothing can be done about it.

How often do we hear similar views within our organizations? "Change is hard," people complain. "It's impossible to make a difference around here." "It's our culture." "It's our leadership." "It's our industry." There is no shortage of explanations to tell us that we should accept the way things are.

In this kind of environment, the common wisdom becomes, "Don't try to be creative or inventive or innovative; don't try to improve the way we do things." Good ideas are neutralized, and great ideas go unrecognized. People's natural desire to get involved is continuously thwarted, so they disengage. Too often, members of the organization assume that they are incapable of having an impact on the situation, and they respond by burying their highest aspirations and deepest values. In this way, many organizations destroy employees' souls without meaning to.

It's a sad truth that people usually *want* the opposite of what they actually *produce*. The most grandiose mission statements, the most pompous vision statements, the most hopeful value statements, the most idealistic platitudes and slogans will not change the fact that an organization's patterns of behavior are caused by the underlying systems and structures that drive those patterns. Without a change of these critical causal factors, change efforts will never last long. Old patterns will reoccur, what is new will be overcome, and the organization will reject the change effort much like a body will reject an implanted organ.

The good news is that real and lasting change, when well motivated, does exist in abundance. Not too many people would go back to an electronic typewriter once they have word processing. Few folks would give up their cell phones, Blackberries, e-mail, text messaging, video conferencing, and plasma HD televisions in favor of phone booths, snail mail, and old black-and-white televisions with only three networks. Change, when appropriately inspired, is more than possible. It is probable.

Yet change takes something special: *organizational learning*. This is a relatively new idea, made popular in Peter Senge's highly acclaimed book, *The Fifth Discipline: The Art & Practice of the Learning Organization* (Doubleday/Currency, 1990). Unfortunately, the term, like many terms within the business context, has been reduced to yet another organizational slogan. I have heard many proclaim about their companies, "We are a learning organization!" Yet the reality is quite different. A lot of learning might have been going on, but it was not *organizational* learning. And here is an important insight that the sheep discover: Individual learning, good as it is, does not necessarily translate into organizational learning. The learning must become *collective*.

Collective learning means that the group (or flock) itself has acquired knowledge, skill, wherewithal, competence, and facility. The organization *itself* contains all of this. If one person leaves, the unit continues to maintain what it has learned. Moreover, it is able to bring new people into a system of collective learning.

Organizational learning is an outcome of an enterprise-wide thought process in which reality can be understood from collective vantage points. Are you seeing what I am? Am I seeing what you are? And when we are seeing things differently, how are we to understand the difference? What are you seeing that I'm not seeing? What am I seeing that you're not seeing? Rather than attempting to determine who is right and who is wrong, we are able to explore reality objectively, collectively, clearly, and from a larger perspective.

Not only that, organizational learning has a definitive purpose: to create desired end results. What is it that we want to bring into being? How can we move from our starting point to our desired ending point? By exploring these previously alien concepts, little by little, the sheep begin to embrace the prospect of a long and happy life.

Often, creative thought springs from the failure of traditional approaches to bring about the results we want. People often explain their complacency by claiming, "We don't have enough time or money." Just what does that mean? It means that we don't have ample resources to accomplish the result in *conventional* ways. So, if we are to accomplish our aims, we must move from convention to *invention*. We are suddenly motivated to create something that hasn't existed before, something new and often unheard of. This becomes an exercise in collective inquiry, collective discovery, collective innovation, and the best example of a collective creative process.

As the sheep learn, mindlessness is always the enemy. And yet, frequently, our institutions are content to encourage a form of mindlessness in the form of tried-and-true policy designs, norms, bad habits, avoidance of truth, commitment to the usual processes, and fixed ways of thinking.

Mindfulness comes from the ability of an organization to rethink *everything*. Why not examine every element with fresh eyes? Why accept common practice or common "wisdom"? Together, a group can be more than the sum of its parts. It can form what in music is called *ensemble*, which is the united performance of an integrated group of people who act with such affinity toward each other and their work that they create something transcendental.

Outlearning the Wolves: Surviving and Thriving in a Learning Organization is a true classic because of the way in which this beautifully told and delightfully illustrated tale reflects the deeper principles of organizational learning. It demonstrates that a good story can be one of the best sources of profound change. When a team, department, or entire organization reads this book together, they can easily see how they can become more effective by following its insights. Everyone can quickly be on the same page, positioned to put these valuable lessons into practice—and, in the process, to rediscover their highest aspirations, for themselves and their organization.

Robert Fritz
Newfane, Vermont
September 2007

Introduction

My conference call isn't going that well. I'm interviewing a group of executives from a Fortune 500 corporation for a learning program on the subject of trust and teamwork in organizations. I'm not getting what I need.

"Trust is a bedrock of effective teams," one of the executives tells me.

"That's a good point," I say as I lean into the phone. "Can you illustrate that with a story?"

Another disembodied voice comes back through the speaker: "You have to establish trust with your actions, and it has to be backed up by systems."

"Great," I say. "Can you give me an example of that or tell me a story—perhaps one about learning that lesson the hard way?"

"Sure," says another. "You have to be authentic. You can't fake trust."

"Yes, but I'm looking for your *stories* . . . ."

And so it goes. The group delivers a series of pointed truisms with efficiency, and their correct answers are all the more credible for having been tested in an intensely competitive, results-driven culture. But I am intrigued by their seeming refusal to articulate their knowledge in the form of a narrative. Is it because they *can't* or they *won't?*

I have to believe this shortcoming is not a matter of capability. It isn't a stretch to imagine these smart, experienced practitioners going home to their families and sitting around the dinner table as their spouses ask how their day went. "Well, I had an interview with this writer guy from Tennessee . . . ." They will pass the green beans, and they will tell stories, as all of us do, because from the dinner table to the campfire to the town square, story is the currency for human communication.

A Path to Learning

So what is it about the corporate setting that often makes it an inhospitable environment for narrative? Would telling stories simply have taken too long for this group of time-crunched executives or perhaps left them too emotionally vulnerable? Would their open-ended tales from the trenches have been too ambiguous for a culture that demanded precision and correct answers? Or have the PowerPoint body snatchers finally assimilated all of us so that we can now speak only in bullet-pointed reductionism?

Ten years ago, I stumbled into the world of organizational storytelling somewhat accidentally, when I wrote a silly story for one of the most influential brands in the world. I developed my tale, which hinged on a group of talking sheep and pop-culture references, as a catalyst for conversations about learning at a Fortune 100 company. I confess that upon submitting the first cartoon-illustrated draft to my client customer, I feared that it would be the end of my employment there. It wasn't. Even though the company ultimately passed on *Outlearning the Wolves* for strategic reasons, I was surprised by the enthusiastic reception that Otto the sheep received in the hallowed halls of that organization. And I was surprised once again when I received a call from a forward-thinking publisher called Pegasus Communications only a couple weeks after I mailed the manuscript to them, unsolicited, in a plain manila envelope.

In the decade that has passed, Otto and his wooly friends have found an enthusiastic worldwide audience that has proven itself willing to surpass me in the practice of play as a path to learning. Oh, I've heard the stories:

- Municipal leaders in the Singapore government initiated conversations about learning within their ranks using sheep puppets.
- Vice presidents in a conservative financial powerhouse donned sheep and wolf noses, acted out the whole adventure, and were even gutsy enough to post the video on their corporate intranet.
- K–12 school leaders played a game based on the story to illuminate different leadership styles and issues.

- Grade-school kids around the world have analyzed, reimagined, and rewritten *Outlearning the Wolves* with new epilogues and exciting possibilities for Otto and his friends.

Indeed, Otto seems to have no fixed audience. He is equally at ease in the graduate-level classroom and my own living room, where my nine-year-old daughter digested the book easily, telling me I did a "pretty good job." (Her praise for her dad, though understated, is nonetheless invaluable because of the infrequency with which she dispenses it.)

Today, more and more people are talking about how stories can be used to create change, build culture, disseminate learning, and capture knowledge. Thinkers like former World Bank vice president Stephen Denning are elevating the discourse with disciplined tomes like *The Leader's Guide to Storytelling: Mastering the Art and Discipline of Business Narrative* (Jossey-Bass, 2005). Some of my colleagues and clients have revised their organizations' leadership competency models to include storytelling as a core capability. And an unmistakable constructivist tone is creeping into the business vernacular: "Markets are conversations," claimed one dramatic online manifesto as it slapped organizations out of their comas and challenged them to find more relevant and human ways of talking with customers and among themselves.

Storytelling is innate and intuitive, and yet I encounter a lot of people who feel anxious about it.

"I don't have the charisma or speaking skills to be a good story-teller," many people tell me.

"Neither do I," I say. "I think it is more important to tell the right story than it is to tell the story well."

"Stories aren't going to fly in my culture," they say.

"I think you will be surprised," I say. "The stories are already in your culture. It's just a matter of recognizing and relaying the right ones to create the future that you desire."

"Storytelling is a soft skill," executives whisper.

I counter: "Storytelling is a solid business discipline that goes to the core of your leadership."

The Right Story

Ultimately, the conversation about organizational narrative turns on a fundamental question: *How do I know which story is the right story?*

That's a tough one.

Sometimes I answer in terms of templates, distinguishing between *stories of identity* and *stories of aspiration and change.* Or perhaps I will challenge the person to start with the desired outcome and identify the existing stories that will help others envision the relevance of that outcome.

Which story is the right story? The real answer is, *I don't fully know. That's where the art comes in.*

I'm hanging out with a friend in an Atlanta club at the end of a corporate learning gig. Though we have left our ties in the car, our slacks and button-down shirts make us indistinguishable from the other working wonks in this Buckhead crowd. My colleague poses a variant on the which-story-is-the-right-story conundrum: "So how do you know when to use the Learning Fables?" he asks. "And how do you know when you should use another approach?"

"I'll show you a way I've been thinking about this," I say. I draw a line across a cocktail napkin, appreciating how this impromptu, beer-stained canvas adds instant drama and credence to my noodlings.

"There really is no end to the kinds of stories that can be used in an organizational setting," I tell him. "I find that I always begin by answering two fundamental questions. The first question is *how close to reality should the story be?* So on the left side of the line are stories that directly reflect the reality that we live in. And on the far right are stories that are very different."

My World ———————————————— Distant Reality

I continue, "On the far left are stories that simply describe the world we live in. For example, they are the stories that companies might tell in their annual reports, citizenship reports, and so on."

My friend points to the middle point of the line. "The learning program we just developed would go here, further over to the right," he says.

I agree. "Yeah, our learning program today was an extended case study. Case studies are drawn from an organizational reality that we all recognize. But some of the details are changed so that people don't get defensive. It's in a distant reality, but not too distant. That's why case studies make great learning tools. They look a lot like our world, but the names and other key details are changed so that, in effect, we can talk about ourselves without actually talking about ourselves."

My colleague's eyes are still tracking along the horizontal line. "Your series of Learning Fables goes all the way over here on the right," he says and points to the "Distant Reality" end of the continuum. "In the Learning Fables, you're using talking animals and fantasy worlds. It looks nothing like our world."

"But it's a metaphor for our world. The audience recognizes that the story has been constructed to tell them something about themselves. By immersing themselves in a world where sheep can talk and where the illustrations look like they were made for a children's book, readers feel invited to relax, be playful, explore, and exercise their imaginations to think expansively. They're not limited by the way things are in their current world. Out in the meadow with the sheep, readers experience the constant threat of the wolves; they can reflect on the feeling of vulnerability that comes with being in a changing world; and they can explore solutions that aren't limited by the rules and structures of their real-world organization. It is very freeing."

We both stop and reflect for a moment. *Stories on the left side lead us to think analytically about what currently is; stories on the right lead us to reflect expansively on what could be. And, of course, there are all varieties of stories in between that accomplish both to varying degrees.*

My friend breaks the silence. "So the first question you ask is how close to reality," he says as he orders another beer. "What is the second?"

"The second is something I always struggle with. I ask *how overtly do I draw out the learnings?*" I draw a vertical line down the napkin; the ink bleeds where the line intersects a beer ring.

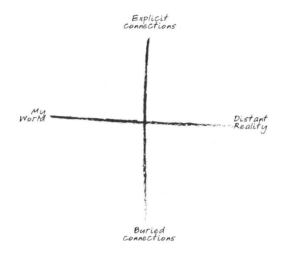

In developing the *Wolves* manuscript, I struggled with the question, *how much of the metaphor do I explain?* At first, I really didn't want to provide any explanation at all, putting my trust in the power of the narrative to stimulate the audience and motivate them to draw their own connections. I eventually backed down from my extreme position, and I'm glad I did. I have learned that when connections remain too buried, audiences may feel a little lost. If the end goal is to create meaning (and not just to entertain), then you have to establish some kind of framework, model, or language. The question is, how much? Draw too many connections, and the audience is robbed of the process of discovery and lateral association; draw too few, and the audience doesn't have enough context to have a meaningful conversation.

Fairy tales, for example, are relatively low on this continuum. Theorists like Bruno Bettelheim argue that the meaning in stories like "Little Red Riding Hood" is deeply buried. It's in there; we just respond to it at a subconscious level.

Aesop's Fables, on the other hand, are higher up on the continuum. There are no hidden connections; they have explicit morals. The audience for "The Tortoise and the Hare," for example, knows that the message of the story is "Slow and steady wins the race." You don't have to dig at all to get the meaning; Aesop makes it easy and just tells you. One could argue that "Little Red Riding Hood" offers a deeper well of meaning than "The Tortoise and the Hare" and is therefore a richer resource for learning. (Indeed, Bettelheim says that, for this very reason, fairy tales are essential for the moral development of children.)

Similarly, the richest organizational stories are the ones that capture the essence of the organization's identity—either "who we are" or "who we will become"—but also contain enough ambiguity, frayed edges, and unresolved plot threads and metaphors so that there is still plenty of meaning for organizational members to unpack. With the Learning Fables, I am continually mindful of drawing out the meaning in bites that are just the right size. The stories are followed by a short piece that initiates the meaning-making process, but then hands it over and says, *"Your turn."* Big questions about the metaphor are posed but never conclusively answered. (One of my favorites: *In your organization, what do the wolves represent?*)

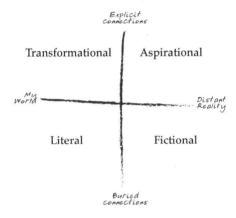

So which stories are most effective in organizations? The answer is *all of them* (see "David Hutchens' Storytelling Matrix"). Start anywhere on the horizontal axis, depending on whether you want descriptive stories of your current reality or stories that can be catalysts for new ways of thinking because they are fixed in a distant reality. Then, "move upward" and have conversations to draw out the meaning of those stories. Because while the first purpose of the story in a movie or novel is to provide entertainment and escape, in organizations it is to create *change*. And the possibility of change grows only when the story has engaged people's imaginations, invited them to reflect upon the story's meaning, and moved them to respond with stories of their own.

David Hutchens' Storytelling Matrix

- **The Realm of the Literal.** These are descriptive stories that exist in the present reality with buried connections.
  - *The role of the storyteller* is to describe or report on reality.
  - *The role of the audience* is to assimilate the story and add it to their current understanding of the world.
  - *Examples include* news reports, organizational annual reports.
- **The Realm of the Fictional.** These are stories that take place in a distant reality and have buried connections.
  - *The role of the storyteller* is to engage and entertain.
  - *The role of the audience* is to surrender and trust the story to take them on a journey that they will find rewarding.
  - *Examples include* fairy tales, movies like *Star Wars*, Greek myths.
- **The Realm of the Transformational.** These are stories that take place in the present reality with the connections made explicit.
  - *The role of the storyteller* is to editorialize, scrutinize, or judge.
  - *The role of the audience* is to analyze and participate in the meaning-making conversation.
  - *Examples include* case studies, books like *The One Minute Manager*.
- **The Realm of the Aspirational.** These are stories in a distant reality with the connections made explicit.
  - *The role of the storyteller* is to suggest connections to the story's metaphors.
  - *The role of the audience* is to continue the work established by the storyteller and draw additional connections between the story and their reality. In this way, the audience becomes a "co-storyteller" in the ongoing creation of the story.
  - *Examples include* the "Learning Fables" books, religious parables, *Who Moved My Cheese*.

Your Stories

So where does *Outlearning the Wolves* go from here? Given the potential of stories—any story—to create new meaning in your organization, I say with all sincerity and conviction that that depends on you. My hope is that your exploration of stories won't end with Otto the Sheep, Sparky the Penguin, and the others, but that you would continue drawing connections between their stories and *your* story. The ultimate application occurs when you re-live and also create your own true stories of learning . . . and then share them with others in your organization. If you wish to embark on the journey of organizational learning, I can think of no better way to begin than with these words: "I'd like to tell you a story . . . ."

The First Chapter

This is a wolf.

This is a sheep.

Wolves eat sheep.

Any questions?

Wolves have always eaten sheep.
They always will eat sheep.
If you are a sheep, you accept this as a fact of life.

A flock of sheep once lived together in a beautiful, green pasture.

But the flock's existence was not a peaceful one. The wolves posed a constant threat, casting a shadow of fear over the pasture.

Sometimes, the flock would settle in to sleep at night and awake in the morning to find that one of them was gone—likely being served up to a wolf with asparagus tips and mint jelly.

There were several miles of sharp, barbed-wire fence that surrounded the sheep's fields.

But the wolves came anyway.

It was hard to live amid such uncertainty.

Still, over the years, the flock got bigger and bigger and bigger. The occasional loss, though very sad, was to be expected.

This was the way
it had always been.

Another Chapter

This is Otto.

You should know that Otto will face an untimely demise by the end of this story.

Don't get too attached to him.

Otto was saddened by the rest of the flock's resignation to the wolves.

"I have a dream . . . " said Otto, perched on a hill where the rest of the flock could hear him. "I dream of a day when not another sheep will ever die to become breakfast for a wolf."

"That is absurd," said Shep the sheep. "You cannot stop the wolf. Remember the inspiring words of our ancestors: '*The wolf will come, just as the sun will rise.*' And also: '*Wolves. What jerks.*'"

"Indeed, I believe we are to be *commended*," said another sheep. "For we have prospered beneath the shadow of the wolf. Just look at how many of us there are!"

This made Otto even sadder.

"As long as the wolf is present, our strong numbers tell us only a half-truth," said Otto. "We tell ourselves we are strong so we won't have to face up to the ways we are weak."

Otto continued: "We all say the wolf cannot be stopped. But how do we *know* this is true?"

A sheep named Curly answered, "It *is* true. Why, even the fence that surrounds us cannot keep the wolves away. At first, it stopped them. But they must have learned to jump over it. Wolves learn very quickly," Curly added.

"Then *we* must learn—even more quickly!" said Otto. "We must make learning an ongoing part of life in the flock. We will become a *learning* flock."

"But we *do* learn," said Shep, mildly indignant. "Why, just the other day, I learned to pull a thorn out of my hoof with my teeth." (All the other sheep—especially those with thorns in their hooves—raised their woolly eyebrows in interest.)

"And I have learned to dig a hole. Watch this!" said Gigi, as she began vigorously clawing at the ground.

"Uh . . . I can push rocks around with my nose to make a pile," offered Jerome, who was just barely following the conversation.

An excited murmur arose among the sheep at these new insights, which, though perhaps obvious to you and me, were quite innovative and useful in the sheep world.

"This learning is a good start," said Otto, a little encouraged. "Ideas like these must be shared for the benefit of the flock."

"But to thrive in the shadow of the wolf, it is not enough. We need a different kind of learning if we are to be a true learning flock."

The flock looked down, sheepishly. They were trying hard to understand.

After some silence, Curly spoke. "Perhaps we could sleep in a circle."

Otto motioned for her to continue.

"Well," said Curly, "I think we could protect ourselves better if we slept in a huddle and not scattered all over the place. That way, when the wolves come, it will be harder for them to get us."

"But that doesn't really address the problem of the wolves . . . " said Marietta, a little lamb. But no one heard her. The sheep were too excited by Curly's idea.

"Yes, yes!" they all said. "Tonight we will huddle against the wolves. *Learning* may be a good idea after all!"

Otto was frustrated by the sheep's attempt at learning, which, to him, seemed awfully reactionary. But he felt relieved to see them at least united in purpose. This was a good first step. "The least I can do," he thought, "is stay awake tonight and keep guard while they sleep."

(WARNING! This brings us to the part of the story where Otto cashes in his chips. Take comfort in knowing that he is going to a better place where he will join Lassie, Old Yeller, and Bambi's mother.)

That night, Otto watched as the sky darkened and the sheep gathered together into a huddle. By the time the crescent moon was high in the summer sky, the flock had fallen fast asleep.

The next morning, Otto was gone.

Yet Another Chapter

When the flock woke the next morning to find Otto gone, they were devastated.

"Otto was a good sheep," sighed Shep.

"He showed us a vision of a better day," eulogized Curly.

"He had fleece as white as snow," someone said from the back.

Jerome didn't say anything. He just pushed a bunch of rocks into a pile with his nose—perhaps not the most effective coping mechanism, but it seemed to work for him.

But the mood soon turned sour.

"Those wolves! This is all their fault!" moaned Curly.

"What are we supposed to do?" cried Shep. "The wolves are smart, and they are strong, and they cannot be stopped. Our lives would be so much better if there were no wolves."

"If only that stupid fence were taller, so the wolves could not jump over it."

The flock sat there, dejected and miserable.

Finally, Marietta, the little lamb, spoke again.

"How come the wolves only come sometimes, and not all the time?" she asked the flock.

Everyone stopped. They looked confused.

Marietta continued. "If wolves are smart, and they can jump over the fence anytime they want, how come they don't come *every* night? If I were a wolf, that's what *I* would do. I would feast on sheep all the time."

The others looked even more confused.

"All I'm saying," said Marietta, "is that maybe the wolves aren't as unstoppable as we think. *Something* is stopping them, at least some of the time."

"What are you getting at, Marietta?" asked Shep.

"I'm saying the same thing Otto said. We must learn. We must do it together. And we must learn faster than the wolves."

"We tried being a learning flock already," said Shep. "And look where it got Otto."

"That's because we've only just started," said the wise little lamb. "Look at what just happened: We tried something *different,* but the results we got were the same. What does that tell you?"

Everyone had to admit that it was a pretty good question. But no one had an answer.

Marietta explained: "It tells *me* it isn't enough just to change the way we do things. We must also change the way we *see* and the way we *think*. We need to learn *how to learn differently.*"

"How?" everyone wanted to know.

"We can start by doing three things:

"One, remember Otto's vision: *Someday, not another sheep will ever die because of wolves.* If we keep that in mind, I think we'll know what to do.

"Two, let's take stock of what we believe. Everyone says that wolves are too smart, and cannot be stopped. We have made all of our decisions thinking that this is true, and maybe it is. *But what if it isn't?*

"Three, let's figure out how to do things differently. What do we have to do to stop the wolves? What is it like to *be* a wolf? Let's go out and get some ideas and information. Let's find out as much about the wolves as we can. Then, let's share everything we know with each other.

"Why don't we each do some thinking on our own, and then meet here this afternoon to talk?"

The meeting adjourned, and the sheep all went their separate ways, lost in thought.

Some of the sheep struggled with what Marietta had said:

"Learning may be all well and good. But if that fence isn't tall enough to keep out wolves, there is nothing we can do. We don't have the tools to make it taller."

 "I won't stand for this kind of disrespect to our ancestors. They taught us that wolves were a fact of life. That little ewe is making a mockery of our heritage."

But some of the sheep took what Marietta said to heart:

"Marietta is right. The wolves only seem to come at certain times. That doesn't make sense."

"Last summer, when we had the drought, the wolves seemed to come much more often. Hmmmm. . . . "

"Maybe the wolves *aren't* jumping over the fence. It's pretty high . . . and I don't think any animal is *that* strong. . . . "

Later that afternoon, all the sheep came back together to talk. A feeling of excitement buzzed among them. (Impressed by the turnout, Jerome made an attempt to count the sheep . . . but, strangely, he found himself becoming so sleepy that he had to stop.)

Shep began the meeting. "Friends, we are here today in memory of our friend Otto, and his vision to eliminate one hundred percent of deaths due to wolf attacks. Does anybody have anything to share?"

The sheep shared all their thoughts.

They engaged in a deep discussion about whether a wolf could really jump over the fence.

They discussed the strange timing of WRCs (Wolf-Related Casualties), and how they seemed to decrease after hard rains and increase during hot and dry periods.

They even confessed how difficult it was for them to rethink their own long-held beliefs about wolves.

Just talking about these things energized the flock and gave them hope.

Suddenly, Curly came trotting up, out of breath but very excited.

"Follow me! Hurry!" she said.

Confused, the sheep ran off after her, not at all sure where Curly was leading them.

The Final Chapter

The flock hurried after Curly for about a mile.
Soon they came to the fence, right at the spot
where a small stream ran underneath it. This was
the same stream where the sheep often drank—
although never this close to the fence, for fear of
wolves.

"Look!" Curly said, pointing with her hoof to the spot where the fence crossed over the water. There, just above the surface of the water and caught on the barbed wire, was a small clump of sheep's wool.

"I was looking around for answers and I found this—but I don't know what it means," she said.

The sheep looked at each other in confusion.

Finally, someone spoke up. "I got it! The wolves aren't going over the fence. They're going *under* it!"

Another sheep excitedly added, "*That* makes sense! When there is a drought, there is no water going under the fence. That's when the wolves crawl under!"

"And after it rains, there's too *much* water, and the wolves can't go under," exclaimed another.

The sheep got even more excited.

"So I guess that means . . . *wolves can't swim!*" Everyone laughed heartily at this.

Perhaps the wolves weren't so smart after all.

"There's only one problem," someone said. "We can't control when it rains. We're still at the mercy of the wolves. And now we're at the mercy of the weather, too."

The flock fell quiet.

Then Gigi spoke. "I think we're looking at the wrong problem again.

"It's true that we can't control the weather. But we *can* control the flow of the water. Watch this." And Gigi began to dig a hole, vigorously pawing at the ground under the fence with her hooves. Soon, some of the other sheep joined in.

"Don't just stand there! Everybody help!" someone called.

"Well . . . I can push rocks around with my nose to make a pile," Jerome offered, and began building a small dam with rocks, a few feet downstream.

Shep stood by, pulling thorns out of the hooves of other sheep as they dug.

Soon, a small pond began to form around the fence.

Amazed by this achievement, the sheep let out a spontaneous, collective bleating sound (an extremely irritating noise, but it sounds joyful if you're another sheep).

In the days that followed, the flock had a beautiful pond around which they could gather and drink and play.

But best of all, the wolves stopped coming . . .

. . . the sheep stopped disappearing . . .

. . . and the fear was gone.

"I'm glad we became a learning flock," the sheep would later say, as they nestled safely in to sleep at night.

"It feels good to know that we'll never have to go through anything like that ever again."

50

But maybe they would.

The End

Discussion Guide and Questions

What kind of a business book that wanted to communicate serious business theory would do so using cute, talking animals?!

Far too few! After all, having fun can be an important part of learning. And a metaphor, like the one in this book, is a powerful medium through which you can encounter new truths and new possibilities for the world *you* inhabit.

Behind their wisecracks, the sheep in this story have some important ideas to share. These ideas can have a far-reaching impact on the way organizations do business on a global scale, as well as the way you do your work on a day-to-day basis. Let's take a closer look at their experience, and see what lessons you can take home to your *own* flock.

Toward a Learning Culture

Much has been said and written about cultures of *organizational learning*. But what *is* a learning culture? How does one go about creating it? And what is meant by "learning"?

Every organization—whether it is a Fortune 100 firm, a sports team, the government, an elementary school, a church, or even your family—is faced with the challenge of *finding ways to create the results it desires*. Often, an organization must initiate both large and small changes to realize its vision. But change can be difficult. Indeed, in the U.S. publishing industry, the best selling category for nonfiction books is change management. Clearly, questions about these topics abound.

Change happens all the time. It's *easy* to create change. The hard part is creating change that is both *sustaining* and *transformational.* As Otto and Marietta discovered, this kind of change is initiated only when individual people (or sheep) are deeply engaged with the change process, personally and emotionally. This is change that requires *learning.*

So let's return to our question of what learning actually is. *Learning* is continually enhancing one's capability to create, think, relate, and act in productive ways. Learning is innate. You—and your organization—are learning all the time, whether you intend to or not. The big question is, *What can we do to trigger this innate learning ability in ways that help us achieve the things that matter to us the most?*

This is the question Peter Senge addresses with his Learning Organization Framework (also known as the MIT Model.)[1] *Outlearning the Wolves* is built on this model; strip away the wolves, sheep, and story elements, and this is the skeleton you'll find underneath:

The framework suggests there are three domains that create organizational learning. The first, at the far right, is **Results**. This domain addresses the question "Why bother?" What are the measurable and observable outcomes the organization wishes to create? Otto articulated a highly motivating end result when he envisioned "a day when not another sheep will have to die to become breakfast for a wolf." He also said, "We will become a learning flock." Without compelling, clearly defined results, organizational learning does not take place. (It also won't happen if the intended results fail to tap into people's deepest aspirations.)

The Domain of Action is the next area. This is where much organizational theory is focused. It addresses the question *"What* will we do, or put in place, to achieve the results we desire?" Anything you can *plan, do,* or *see* is in the Domain of Action. People

1. Model is from Peter Senge, in *The Fifth Discipline Fieldbook* (Doubleday, 1994), pp. 15–47.

and groups who focus most of their energies here may find that they can indeed produce their desired results—but not for long. Over time, motivation and ability to sustain the changes will lag.

The Domain of Change is the final realm. Also called "The Deep Learning Cycle," this domain addresses the question "How will we pursue our goals in a way *that engages people's hearts and spirits?*" This is the mysterious and oft-ignored "people piece" of the framework. When we create environments where people choose to enroll themselves in the doing, we create the possibility for sustainable, transformational change. Note that you can't *make* someone engage in the deep learning cycle; people can only choose to enter into it themselves. That's why this model is so powerful, and so elusive. If a learning culture takes hold in an organization, it will be because of individuals like you who are committed to learning and growing.

So how did Otto, Marietta, and the rest of the flock create an environment where sheep chose to personally engage in improving their lives? Great question. Let's take a closer look at their experience of the Learning Organization Framework, and see what lessons it might hold for us.

<hr>

Learning and the Domain of Action

Let's begin with the Domain of Action portion of the framework. Whether you are a flock of sheep or a global company, there are three areas in which collective, coordinated action may take place in order for a learning culture to germinate.

•**Guiding Ideas.** This is defined as *the best thinking people have to date about how to achieve the results they desire.* Guiding ideas include the beliefs, assumptions, and values that we hold about what it will take to create a particular desired result. Every organization

Guiding Ideas

Domain of Action

is governed by guiding ideas, whether these are openly stated or not. For example, a company may believe that only by hiring the top R&D engineering talent can it beat its competitors. In the story, the sheep were initially governed by a passive, unspoken guiding idea: We are victims, and merely to survive is success. Marietta broke significant ground when she introduced a radical new guiding idea: *that the flock could achieve the results they desired by first explicitly discussing their beliefs about wolves.* It was a courageous act, just as it is when anyone challenges deeply held convictions. (Remember the sheep who said, "She's making a mockery of our heritage"?) Marietta's new guiding idea catalyzed some powerful new behaviors in the flock.

- **Theory, Methods, and Tools.** These are the reusable, generalized areas of knowledge and practices people can draw upon, usually available in the public domain. They are especially important for testing *new* guiding ideas. In the story, Marietta called a

meeting, in which the sheep gathered around a rock to communicate. Nothing pioneering here; meetings, as a kind of tool, have been around for ages. But for the flock, the introduction of this method accelerated their journey toward their desired result.

- **Innovations in Infrastructure.** Many people think of "structure" as tiered boxes on an organizational chart. But structures are more than that. They are anything that directs resources (energy, time, money, attention, etc.) toward achieving the desired results. Of course, the sheep's pond was one new structure. In the story,

Marietta offered another structure in her speech to the flock: "Let's find out as much about the wolves as we can. Then let's share what we learn with one another." In other words, the sheep's new infrastructure involved an information-gathering and -sharing network. Sure, that's pretty basic. But it is an infrastructure nonetheless. In the sheep's case, this simple innovation produced some dramatic shared learning.

56

The Domain of Change: The Deep Learning Cycle

Organizations learn when people learn. And when people choose learning, they embark on a journey in which the destination is never reached. Yes, they adopt new ways of *doing* things. But more important, they embrace new ways of *being* and *seeing*. For people who engage in this kind of learning, a profound experience often occurs that might be described as an "awakening." Such people literally see the world and their place in it differently.

With this kind of perspective, the flock of sheep in the story ended up creating a pond that kept out the wolves and enhanced the sheep's quality of existence. It was an extraordinary collective achievement. The flock changed because the individual sheep were deeply engaged. Change takes place in three areas:

• **New Skills and Capabilities**. How do people know whether they are learning? Easy. According to Peter Senge, author of *The Fifth Discipline* and coauthor of *The Fifth Discipline Fieldbook* and *The Dance of Change* (three seminal texts on the principles of the learning culture), we know we are learning "when we can do things we couldn't do before." For example, the fact that Jerome learned to push rocks around with his nose was, in fact, legitimate learning. (At least, for him it was.) Transferring that skill into the new context of building a dam to create a pond that would protect the flock from wolves was an even higher level of skill building and learning for Jerome that benefited everyone.

Skills & Capabilities

Domain of Change

• **New Awareness and Sensibilities.** These are enhanced insights, or deeper understandings of the complexity around you that prompt you to question what appears obvious to others. For example, some of the sheep realized that "the wolves don't come after the rain, and they come more often when it is hot and dry."

Wasn't this obvious? Why didn't the sheep realize this sooner? Surely there were many opportunities over the years to observe this pattern. Maybe not. The reason the sheep missed this "obvious" pattern is that it *did not match their picture of reality*. It was only at Marietta's urging to challenge the belief ("We all say the wolves cannot be stopped … *but what if it isn't true?*") that the sheep were able to "see" and then explore this readily available information. It was a new awareness that the flock adopted with great struggle, but it produced a dramatic new future for them.

Skills & Capabilities

Awareness & Sensibilities

Domain of Change

• **New Attitudes and Beliefs**. New awarenesses ultimately lead to new beliefs. At the end of the story, the sheep had a collective realization: *Maybe the wolves aren't so smart after all. Maybe they really can be stopped.* Is it surprising that this new belief radically changed things for the flock? Think about it: The person who lives life believing he could die at any moment has a very different experience of life than the person who believes she is relatively safe from harm. The flock's *beliefs* about the world had a very powerful effect on the way the sheep *experienced* the world. When the way you view the world around you changes, *the world itself changes, too.* The flock's new belief about their world had immediate, tangible results. Their lifestyle ("confidence replaced their fearful existence …"); their future ("wolves stopped coming … sheep stopped disappearing …"); and even the landscape of their pasture all changed. The story is a metaphor for the real power that is available to organizations in which individuals are constantly growing and learning.

Skills & Capabilities

Attitudes & Beliefs

Awareness & Sensibilities

Domain of Change

So Where Do I Begin?

In *The Fifth Discipline,* Peter Senge explores five disciplines at considerable length. These disciplines help organizations develop the *skills* and *capabilities* that kick the domain of change (the deep learning cycle) into gear. Briefly, the five disciplines are:

• **Systems Thinking**. Events in our lives are rarely as simple and direct as they appear. *Systems thinking* is the practical application of *system dynamics*—a field of study that examines the patterns and structures that govern nature, families, the economy, our bodies, companies, and all other dynamic systems. The flock's original cause-and-effect view of the world might be "Wolf gets hungry, wolf eats sheep." But the sheep discovered that a more complex system was in play, whereby variables such as the weather, the wolves' limitations, and the flock's own biases all intersected and influenced one another in complex cause-and-effect relationships. Broader systemic awareness gave the sheep the power to grasp some of these complexities and thus act in more productive ways.

• **Personal Mastery**. Personal mastery is the ability to create the results you want with an economy of means. People with a deep sense of personal mastery are on a life-long journey of self discovery. They are keenly aware of the results they wish to create ("I have a dream …" said Otto [with due respect to Martin Luther King, Jr.]); their current reality (the flock's reactive posture); and the gap between those two states. People who practice the discipline of personal mastery may draw upon a deep, seemingly inexhaustible inner energy to create powerful results. Without a commitment to this discipline, we risk living in a *reactive* orientation, victims of the world around us. (Remember the sheep's complaint, "If only the stupid fence were taller … !") For a closer look at this discipline, explore the Learning Fable titled *The Lemming Dilemma: Living with Purpose, Leading with Vision.*

• **Mental Models**. A mental model is a deeply held vision or set of beliefs and assumptions about how the world works. All of us have mental models; it is impossible *not* to have them. As we build mental models about ourselves and our world, these ways of seeing and thinking become more and more ingrained, until it becomes extremely difficult to perceive things in any other way. Ultimately, our experience of the world will begin to change to conform to our beliefs. Again, the flock's belief that the wolves were unstoppable is a powerful example of how mental models can affect the way we experience the world. Ironically, as long as the sheep *believed* the wolves to be unstoppable, they actually *were* unstoppable.

Mental models hold a great deal of power over us. However, in a learning culture, individuals can release the fierce need to defend and justify their mental models and become adept at challenging and "trying on" new ones. Exploring yours and others' is a great way to gain new insights and build a broader understanding of the complex world around you. For a closer look at this discipline, explore the Learning Fable titled *Shadows of the Neanderthal: Illuminating the Beliefs That Limit Our Organizations*.

• **Shared Vision**. Senge says, "When there is genuine vision (as opposed to the all-too-familiar 'vision statement') people excel and learn, not because they are told to, but because they want to." Building true shared vision has been the challenge of leadership over the ages. Too often, leaders generate *compliance* ("I'm just here to do my job ... ") as opposed to true, committed *enrollment* ("I share the organization's goal, and I'll do anything to achieve it.") So how did Otto generate such strong commitment to his vision? A primary factor was that *the vision tapped into the sheep's own deepest aspirations*—in this case, the desire to live free of fear. That's a pretty compelling vision. You can see how it would generate very different results than a jargony "vision statement" to "increase quality, excellence, etc."

• **Team Learning**. True team learning occurs when individuals within a system are aligned in a free-flowing whole as they work together. Groups that have achieved this heightened state describe it in almost mystical terms. Sports teams may call it "being in the flow"; a jazz ensemble may speak of "hitting the groove," in which the music comes not "from you" but "through you." Perhaps you have had this experience in a work team in which all the members were deeply engaged in the task; you felt energized despite exhaustive work, and the output was far greater than you could have created by working individually. The phenomenon of an organization accomplishing something extraordinary (like sheep creating a pond) requires a deep, transformational *dialogue* in which team members can align in new, shared awareness about themselves and the world.

Questions for Reflection and Discussion

The above descriptions offer just a glimpse at the disciplines that may come together to enable the emergence of a learning culture. And now we're back to the original question: *So where do I begin?* Profound change can come from individual reflection as well as from conversations with others. Here are a few ideas to get you started exploring your own thoughts about the concepts in this book:

- *Draw from your own experience.* Think of a time when you felt completely aligned with a work team, your family, or some other group or community, when the energy was flowing, and the group achieved spectacular results. What was it about that experience that allowed this flow to occur?
- *Examine your own mental models.* What is your equivalent to "The wolves can't be stopped"?
- *Think about ideas.* Which ideas in this story and discussion guide do you find most compelling, and why?
- *Learn more.* Would you like to know more about the possibilities of the learning culture? Find out more about it. Peter Senge's *The Fifth Discipline* is a great place to start.

Often, exploring new understandings with others can powerfully enhance learnings that we gain through individual reflection. In that spirit, here are some questions designed to get you talking with your colleagues about the concepts in this book, and thinking about how to use them to make a difference in your own organization. Note: When we use the word *organization* in these questions, we mean your team, department, or entire company. Feel free to explore these questions together on any or all of those levels.

- How might the metaphor in *Outlearning the Wolves* apply to your own organization's ways of doing things?
- Has your organization stated the *results* it is trying to achieve? If so, how do the intended results tap into your own aspirations?
- Look again at the domain-of-action model (pp. 55–56). This model represents "organizational architecture," or those structures that shape how an organization does things. What are some guiding ideas at work in your own organization? How do these ideas influence the theories, methods, and tools used in the organization, and the infrastructures established? Now discuss some possible new guiding ideas to introduce into your organizational "architecture."
- Look at the domain-of-change model described on pp. 57–58. What does it mean to engage people in the deep learning cycle? How does your organization make it attractive for individuals to choose to enter into this cycle?
- How might the five disciplines help your organization develop new skills and capabilities within the learning cycle?

Remember, learning is a journey. It is not a skill or a technique; it is a discipline. It's a way of looking at the world. It is about growth and discovery.

The sheep came together to create a peaceful and prosperous existence, centered on a serene pond in a meadow.

What reality would *you* like to create?

Other Titles by Pegasus Communications

Learning Fables
The Lemming Dilemma: Living with Purpose, Leading with Vision
Shadows of the Neanderthal: Illuminating the Beliefs That Limit Our Organizations
The Tip of the Iceberg: Managing the Hidden Forces That Can Make or Break Your Organization
Listening to the Volcano: Conversations That Open Our Minds to New Possibilities

The Pegasus Workbook Series
Systems Archetype Basics: From Story to Structure
Systems Thinking Basics: From Concepts to Causal Loops

The "Billibonk" Jungle Mysteries
Billibonk & the Thorn Patch   *Frankl's "Thorn Patch" Fieldbook*
Billibonk & the Big Itch   *Frankl's "Big Itch" Fieldbook*

Human Dynamics
Human Dynamics: A New Framework for Understanding People and Realizing the Potential in Our Organizations

The Pegasus Anthology Series
Reflections on Creating Learning Organizations
Managing the Rapids: Stories from the Forefront of the Learning Organization
The New Workplace: Transforming the Character and Culture of Our Organizations
Organizational Learning at Work: Embracing the Challenges of the New Workplace
Making It Happen: Stories from Inside the New Workplace

Newsletters
THE SYSTEMS THINKER®
LEVERAGE POINTS® for a New Workplace, New World

The Innovations in Management Series
Concise, practical volumes on systems thinking and organizational learning tools, principles, and applications.

PEGASUS COMMUNICATIONS, INC. is dedicated to providing resources that help people explore, understand, articulate, and address the challenges they face in managing the complexities of a changing world. Since 1989, Pegasus has worked to build a community of organizational learning practitioners through newsletters, books, audio and video tapes, and its annual *Systems Thinking in Action*® Conference and other events. For more information, contact us at either address below:

One Moody Street
Waltham, MA 02453 USA
Phone: (800) 272-0945 / (781) 398-9700
Fax: (781) 398-7175

www.pegasuscom.com